Building Bridges

**MARLA HUNTER
[HOOPER]**

BUILDING BRIDGES

CONTENTS

To my Husmane, **Khafre**, and my Mummie, **Dr. Marcia Hunter**—your love and unwavering support makes everything possible.

To **Alice Faye Duncan**, my incredible high school librarian, author, and mentor—thank you for encouraging me to just write. Your guidance planted the seeds for this book long before I even knew it.

To **everyone who pre-ordered this book** and those who took the time to read each chapter, providing invaluable feedback—you helped shape this work in ways I can't express.

And to my **couster**, Stephanie "Alyrical" Gowdy—your generosity in bringing this book to life through your illustrations is beyond words. Thank you for believing in this project as much as I do.

This book is a reflection of love, community, and the bridges we build together. Thank you all for being part of this journey.

| 1 |

Introduction: The Rhythm of Inclusion

W elcome!

You've picked up this book because you believe in the power of creating a world where everyone feels seen, heard, and valued. Whether you're an educator shaping young minds, a leader in an organization fostering equity, or someone ready to deepen your commitment to inclusion, this journey is for you.

At its heart, this work isn't about ticking boxes or following trends. It's about something much deeper: **building bridges** that connect us to one another with love, understanding, and action. And just like music, these bridges are built on rhythm, harmony, and grace.

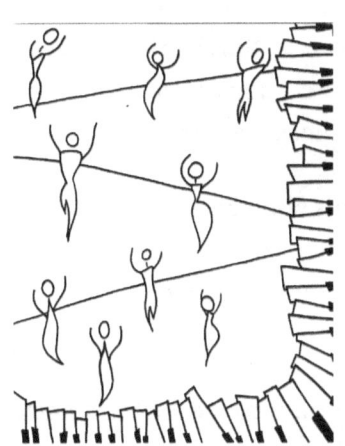

This book isn't just a book—it's a space for you to create, reflect, and grow. Think of it as your personal toolkit, designed for whatever you need:

- **A Creative Outlet:** Use the illustrations as a coloring book to unwind and spark your imagination.
- **A Journal:** Jot down your thoughts, reflect on your journey, and write your story.
- **A Thought Collector:** Capture ideas, inspirations, and plans as you move through the chapters.
- **A Companion:** Return to these pages whenever you need guidance, encouragement, or a spark of creativity.

In the pages ahead, you'll find stories, practical strategies, and moments of reflection designed to inspire and guide you. You'll also discover a curated song for each chapter that creates a playlist, because music has the unique power to unite us, uplift us, and remind us of our shared humanity.

Here's what you can expect:

- **Stories and Examples**: From classrooms in Kenya to boardrooms in Brazil, we'll explore how DEIB principles are transforming lives worldwide.
- **Practical Tools**: Action steps and templates to help you bring these concepts to life in your unique context.
- **A Spirit of Encouragement**: This is a journey, not a race. You don't have to get it all right—you just have to show up and keep growing.

Let this book be your guide, your companion, and your creative space. Whether you're coloring, journaling, reflecting, or simply dreaming, know that every step you take is building a brighter, more inclusive world.

Let's lean into the rhythm together.

Playlist Song: "Lean on Me" – Bill Withers

Your DEIB Playlist

Music connects us on a deep, emotional level, much like the principles of DEIB. Take a moment to create your own "DEIB Playlist" by choosing three songs that resonate with your personal journey. These songs might reflect your hopes, your experiences, or the world you want to help build.

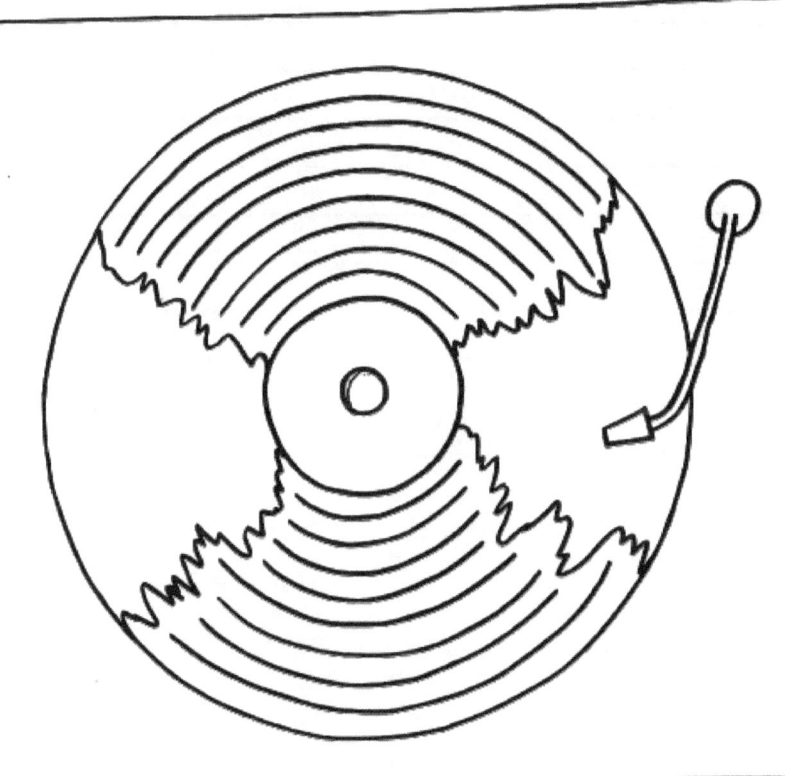

Reflection:

1. What do these songs mean to you in the context of diversity, equity, inclusion, and belonging?
2. How do the themes or lyrics of these songs connect to your personal or professional life?

_____

_____

_____

_____

_____

_____

_____

_____

_____

_____

_____

_____

| 2 |

Diversity is the Melody

Diversity is the Melody

The Power of Diversity

Think about your favorite song. Maybe it's a symphony with a hundred instruments weaving together, or a simple acoustic tune with a melody that touches your heart. Whatever it is, the magic lies in the combination of different sounds. That's what diversity is—bringing together unique voices, experiences, and perspectives to create something beautiful.

But in too many schools, workplaces, and communities, the melody is incomplete. Diverse voices are missing or muted. Our challenge is to make space for every note and ensure that everyone can add their unique sound to the mix.

A Global Perspective on Diversity

Diversity looks different around the world, but its value is universal.

- **In Kenya**: A rural school celebrates diversity by hosting storytelling nights where students share folktales from their tribes, building respect and understanding across cultural lines.
- **In Finland**: Teachers design individualized learning plans, recognizing the diversity of students' needs and abilities.
- **In India**: Schools are blending traditional curricula with environmental education, honoring the country's deep cultural connection to the land.

What does diversity look like in your classroom, workplace, or community? Are certain voices missing from the conversation? How can you make space for them?

Playlist Song: "We Are Family" – Sister Sledge

Spot the Melody in Your Space

Take a moment to look around your environment.

- Who is represented in your books, posters, and materials?
- Whose perspectives are reflected in your lessons or meetings?
- Who might be missing?

Why Diversity Matters

Diversity isn't just about representation—it's about transformation. Studies show that diverse teams solve problems faster, diverse classrooms foster empathy and critical thinking, and diverse voices in media enrich our understanding of the world.

When we embrace diversity, we create spaces where everyone feels they belong and where everyone can thrive.

"Diversity is the mix. Inclusion is making the mix work." – Andrés Tapia

An Orchestra of Voices in Brazil

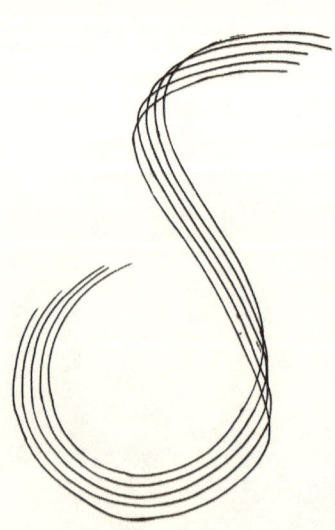

At a school in Rio de Janeiro, a music teacher realized her students came from incredibly diverse cultural backgrounds, but their music curriculum focused solely on European composers. She decided to change that.

Each student brought in a song from their family's cultural heritage. They explored samba, indigenous chants, Afro-Brazilian drumming, and more. The final performance wasn't perfect, but it was magical—a symphony of voices that celebrated the students' roots and connected them to one another.

Dr. Muhammad (2020) emphasizes the importance of centering students' identities and histories in teaching. She introduces a framework where literacy is not just about skills but also about understanding cultural and historical contexts.

"Culturally and historically responsive education allows us to center the knowledge of marginalized communities."

Keep in mind that diversity in classrooms, workplaces, and life mirrors this principle. It's about ensuring that everyone's background and contributions are seen as integral to the larger melody.

How does your current environment celebrate the cultural and historical identities of its members? Where might these identities need more recognition?

Let's try a Global Perspective.
Epeli Hau'ofa (*Our Sea of Islands*):
Hau'ofa, a Pacific Islander scholar, highlights the interconnectedness of Pacific cultures and challenges colonial perspectives that diminish their diversity.

By viewing diversity through this lens, we can reimagine our classrooms and workplaces as interconnected spaces where each person's culture enriches the whole.

Now, think about how interconnectedness shows up in your environment. How can fostering connections across diverse identities create a richer learning or working experience?

Next Steps

This week, find one way to bring more diversity into your work:

- **In a classroom**: Add a book, song, or perspective that reflects a student's background.
- **In a workplace**: Invite someone with a different perspective to lead a discussion or share their experience.
- **In your personal life**: Seek out stories, music, or art from a culture you want to learn more about.

Diversity is the melody, but inclusion is the harmony.

Let's make space for every voice

Spot the Melody

Every environment has its unique melody of diversity, but sometimes certain notes go unheard. Take a moment to reflect on how your classroom, workplace, or community currently celebrates diversity and where there's room for growth.

"We Are Family" – Sister Sledge

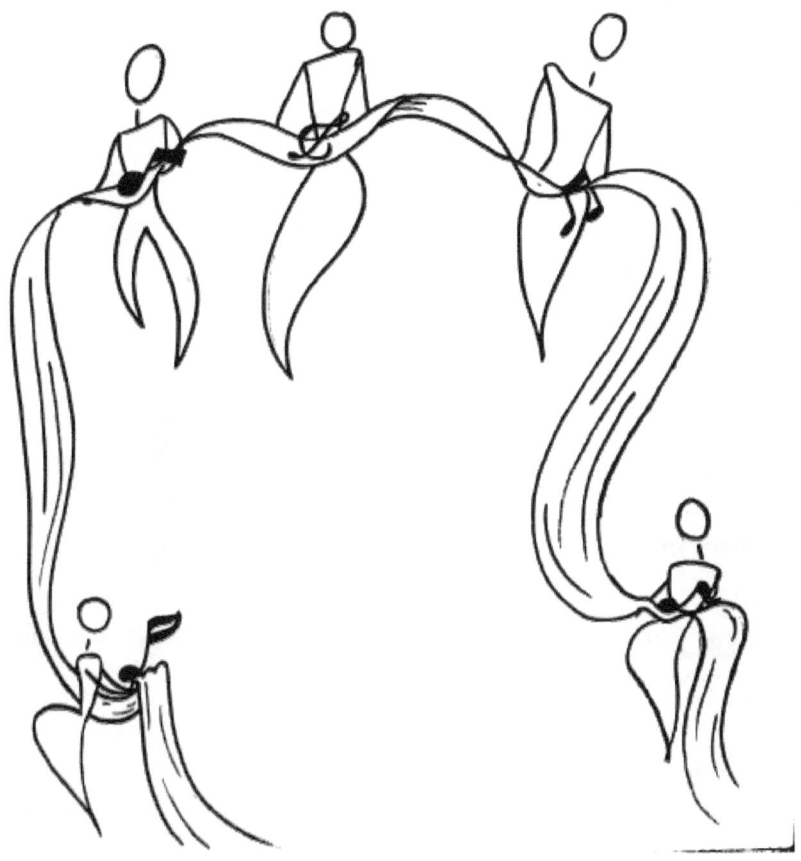

Spot the Melody

Celebrates Diversity	Areas for Improvement
Example: We include diverse authors in our reading list.	Example: Need more diverse voices in STEM materials.

Reflection:

1. How do the areas where diversity is celebrated make your environment stronger?

2.   What small steps can you take to address the areas that need
     improvement?

| 3 |

Equity is the Bridge

Equity is the Bridge

What is Equity?

Equity isn't about treating everyone the same—it's about giving each person what they need to thrive. Picture a bridge. For some people, it's an easy walk. For others, there are gaps, missing planks, or barriers in the way. **Equity is about building that bridge so everyone can make it across safely.**

Unlike equality, which assumes everyone starts from the same place, equity acknowledges that not all bridges are built equally. It's about recognizing those gaps and doing the work to close them.

A Global Perspective on Equity

Here are practices we **should be doing globally** to promote equity:

1. **Providing Essential Resources:**

    ○ Ensure students and employees have access to basic tools like technology, food, and transportation.

    ○ For example, schools can offer after-hours access to computers or provide free meals to students in need.

2. **Removing Systemic Barriers**:

  ○ Identify policies that disproportionately disadvantage certain groups and make them equitable.
  ○ For example, reassess hiring or promotion practices to ensure everyone has an equal chance to succeed.

3. **Incorporating Diverse Knowledge**:

  ○ Collaborate with local communities to integrate culturally relevant practices and knowledge.
  ○ For example, educators can include indigenous perspectives and traditions in their lessons.

4. **Providing Individualized Support**:

  ○ Tailor programs to meet specific needs instead of using a one-size-fits-all approach.
  ○ For example, create individualized learning plans for students with diverse abilities or backgrounds.

Playlist Song: "Man in the Mirror" – Michael Jackson

What barriers to success might exist in your classroom, workplace, or community? What would it look like to remove or reduce those barriers?

Use the area below to collect your thoughts.

Why Equity Matters

When we prioritize equity, we create environments where every person feels supported, valued, and empowered to reach their full potential. For students, this means ensuring they have the tools to succeed—not just academically, but emotionally and socially. For organizations, it means designing systems that uplift underrepresented voices and promote true inclusion.

"Equity is giving everyone what they need to succeed. Equality is treating everyone the same." – Author Unknown

Closing the Gap in South Africa

At a Cape Town school, teachers noticed that many students from low-income households struggled with homework because they lacked internet access. Instead of penalizing those students, the school created an after-hours program where students could use school computers and receive tutoring.

One teacher shared, "It wasn't just about giving them resources. It was about listening to what they needed and showing them they mattered."

The result? Test scores improved, and students reported feeling more confident and included in their learning environment.

Building Equity in Your Space

Step 1: Listen and Observe
Take time to notice where inequities exist.

- Are certain students struggling more than others?
- Are there systemic barriers holding people back in your organization?

Step 2: Take Action

- **For Educators**: Provide alternative ways for students to complete assignments if resources are an issue.
- **For Organizations**: Reevaluate policies that may unintentionally exclude or disadvantage certain groups.

Step 3: Keep the Conversation Going

- Equity isn't a one-time fix. It requires ongoing dialogue, reflection, and adjustment.

Map Your Bridge

Think about your classroom, workplace, or community. What does your "bridge" look like?

- What gaps exist for your students, colleagues, or team members?
- What steps can you take to fill these gaps?

A digital **Bridge Mapping Template** has been created for you. Scan the QR code below to access it in Google Docs. This interactive template will help you identify gaps, plan actions, and track progress.

Dr. Ladson-Billings (1995) argues that equity-focused teaching goes beyond academic success—it also fosters cultural competence and critical consciousness.

"Culturally relevant pedagogy sees students' culture as an asset, not a deficit."

Remember that equity is not just about providing resources—it's about acknowledging and building on the cultural strengths of individuals.

Think about it...

What cultural strengths exist in your classroom or workplace that you can amplify? How can these strengths bridge gaps in access and opportunity?

Let's try a Global Perspective.

Moreton-Robinson (2015), an Aboriginal scholar, explores how systemic inequities are tied to historical structures of power.

Addressing equity requires dismantling systemic barriers. In classrooms, this could mean rethinking disciplinary policies; in workplaces, it could mean equitable hiring practices.

Action Step:

- Identify one systemic barrier in your environment and brainstorm actionable steps to remove it.

Next Steps

This week, choose one small gap to close. Maybe it's providing extra support to a struggling student, reevaluating hiring practices in your workplace, or simply having a conversation about equity with your team. Small actions create big change.

Playlist Song: "Man in the Mirror" – Michael Jackson

Let's build the bridge—together.

Bridging the Gap – A Reflection Journal

I magine equity as a bridge you're building, plank by plank, to connect people to the resources and opportunities they need. Use this journal prompt to reflect on what this bridge looks like in your classroom, workplace, or community.

Your Journal Entry: Bridging the Gap

Date: _____

Prompt 1:
Describe someone in your environment (a student, colleague, or community member) who might be struggling to cross the "bridge" to success. What barriers are they facing?

_____

_____

_____

_____

_____

Date: _____

Prompt 2:

Imagine you're building a bridge for this person. What tools, support, or resources do they need? What first step can you take to help them feel supported?

_____

_____

_____

_____

_____

_____

Date: _____

Prompt 3:

How do you feel when you think about helping others build their bridges? What challenges might you face, and how can you overcome them?

_____

_____

_____

_____

_____

_____

Reflection Song: "Man in the Mirror" – Michael Jackson

Building bridges isn't just about fixing gaps—it's about creating connection, trust, and opportunity. Reflect on how this work changes not just others, but you as well.

| 4 |

Inclusion is the Dance Floor

Inclusion is the Dance Floor

Inclusion is the party where everyone is invited to dance—not just to watch, but to move freely, fully, and authentically. It's about creating spaces where everyone feels welcome, valued, and encouraged to bring their whole selves to the floor.

Playlist Song: "Happy" – Pharrell Williams

What is Inclusion?

Inclusion isn't just about inviting people to the party—it's about making sure everyone feels comfortable joining in. It's about removing barriers that keep people from dancing and creating a culture where individuality is celebrated, not just tolerated.

Think about the last time you felt truly included. It likely wasn't just because you were present—it was because you were seen, heard, and appreciated for who you are. That's what inclusion looks like on the dance floor of life.

A Global Perspective on Inclusion

Around the world, people are redefining what it means to belong:

- **In New Zealand**: Imagine schools incorporating Māori greetings, songs, and cultural practices into the curriculum, ensuring that indigenous students see their culture reflected in daily life.
- **In Japan**: Wouldn't it be wonderful when companies are adopting inclusive hiring practices to welcome neurodiverse employees, providing tailored support to help them thrive.

- **In Ghana**: Community-based schools designing lesson plans that incorporate local traditions, allowing students to connect their education to their cultural roots.

Scholarly Insight:

Dr. Kimberlé Crenshaw (*Mapping the Margins: Intersectionality, Identity Politics, and Violence against Women of Color*):
Dr. Crenshaw's work on intersectionality highlights that true inclusion requires understanding how overlapping identities—like race, gender, and ability—shape experiences of inclusion and exclusion.

If inclusion doesn't account for intersectionality, it risks leaving people behind.
Inclusion is not one-size-fits-all. It's about creating spaces that honor the complexity of everyone's identities.

Story: A Dance Floor in Brazil

At a community center in São Paulo, an educator noticed that some students were reluctant to participate in group activities. Through open conversations, she learned that language barriers were holding them back.

Instead of sticking to traditional methods, she introduced dance as a universal language. Students shared moves from their cultural backgrounds, creating a vibrant, inclusive atmosphere where everyone felt free to express themselves.

The result? A dance floor that wasn't just about movement—it was about connection, confidence, and joy.

What barriers might exist in your environment that prevent people from fully participating? What steps can you take to make your "dance floor" more inclusive?

Use the space below to jot your thoughts down.

Next Steps

This week, take one small step to make your environment more inclusive. Maybe it's inviting someone to collaborate who hasn't had the chance before, or asking what someone needs to feel more included. Small changes create ripple effects.

Playlist Song: "Happy" – Pharrell Williams

Set the Dance Floor

Goal: Help you to envision and create an inclusive environment where everyone feels welcome and valued.

Instructions:

1. **Reflection Prompt:**
   Imagine your classroom, workplace, or community as a dance floor.

   - *Who's on the dance floor right now?*
   - *Who might be sitting on the sidelines?*
   - *What's stopping them from joining in?*

2. **Task 1: Design Your Dance Floor:**
   Use the space below to draw or describe your ideal inclusive dance floor. Think about:

   - Who's dancing (ages, abilities, cultures, etc.).
   - The music playing and how it reflects everyone's preferences.
   - How the space encourages participation.

   What's Happening on the Dance Floor?

Reflection:

1. *What are three specific actions you can take to ensure your "dance floor" is inclusive for everyone?*

_____

_____

_____

_____

_____

2. *How will you know if someone feels included? How can you check in with them to be sure?*

_____

_____

_____

_____

3. *What would it feel like for you to step onto someone else's "dance floor"? What would you need to feel welcomed?*

_____

_____

_____

_____

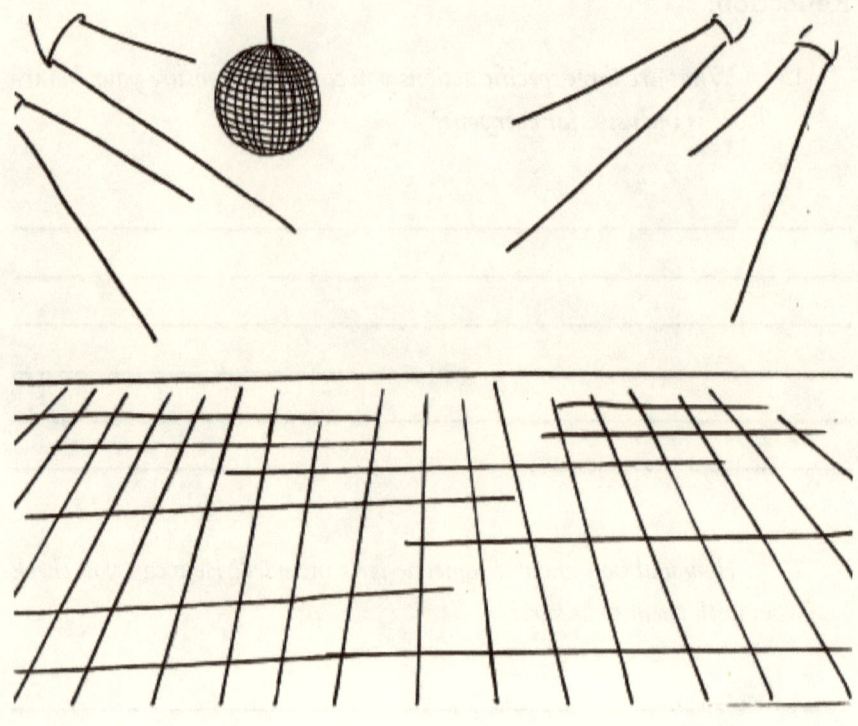

Commit to one actionable step this week to create an inclusive space in your classroom, workplace, or community. Write it here:

My Step:

"Happy" – *Pharrell Williams*

| 5 |

Belonging is the Harmony

Belonging is the Harmony

Belonging isn't just about being included—it's about feeling the harmony of being valued for who you truly are. When we belong, we contribute to something bigger than ourselves, just like voices coming together in a song. Each voice is unique, but every voice is essential to the melody.

What is Belonging?

Belonging happens when people feel genuinely seen and accepted—not in spite of their differences, but because of them. It's about creating an environment where everyone knows they matter and their contributions are vital to the group.

Think about a choir. If even one voice is missing, the harmony feels incomplete. Belonging is ensuring that every voice is present, celebrated, and part of the song.

A Global Perspective on Belonging

Belonging looks different across the world, but its power is universal:

- **In Samoa:** The fa'a Samoa, "The Samoan Way", emphasizes communal values, ensuring that everyone feels connected and supported in the family and community.
- **In Canada:** Indigenous communities use storytelling circles to ensure that everyone's voice is heard and valued, fostering deep connection and belonging.

- **In India**: Schools often hold cultural days where students share their traditions, creating spaces of mutual respect and pride.

Dr. powell (2012), a leading scholar on belonging and inclusion, defines belonging as a practice of deep connection: *"Belonging means being able to participate fully in the life of society—it requires mutual care and accountability."*

We need to understand that belonging is about ensuring everyone has the opportunity to contribute and feel valued. It's not just about access; it's about fostering a sense of purpose and connection within the group.

Think about it...

How does your environment create space for mutual care and accountability? Where can it improve?

Jot down your thoughts.

Let's try a Global Perspective

Let's imagine: At an Auckland school, a teacher started a choir with students from different cultural backgrounds. Instead of singing traditional Western songs, each student contributed a song from their own culture. The group learned new languages, rhythms, and melodies, creating a harmonious blend that reflected every voice.

One student shared, "For the first time, I feel like my culture is a part of the school."

The choir became a symbol of belonging, where every voice added depth to the harmony.

Reflection

Think about a time when you felt like you truly belonged. What made that moment special? How can you recreate that feeling for others in your environment?

Belonging happens when we embrace the unique contributions of others and honor them as essential to the bigger picture. This week, take one step to make someone in your community feel they belong.

Playlist Song: "A Change is Gonna Come" – Sam Cooke

Write the Lyrics of Belonging

Goal: Help you reflect on the concept of belonging by writing your own "lyrics" for what belonging means to you and how you can foster it for others.

Instructions:

Imagine you're writing a song about belonging. Each verse represents a way you can create harmony and connection in your environment.

1. **Start with Reflection**:
    Take a moment to think about what belonging feels like to you. Close your eyes and picture a time when you felt truly valued and connected.
2. **Write Your Lyrics**:

    ○   Use the space below to write 3 verses for your "Belonging Song."
    ○   Each verse should focus on a different aspect of belonging:

        ▪   **Verse 1**: What does belonging feel like?
        ▪   **Verse 2**: How can you create belonging for others?
        ▪   **Verse 3**: What actions can you take to sustain belonging in your community?

Write Your Belonging Song Below

Verse 1:

Verse 2:

Verse 3:

Reflection:

How do your "lyrics" reflect the unique contributions you bring to your environment? How can you use these insights to help others feel they belong?

Harmony Journal:

Write down the names of 3 people in your life who might feel disconnected. Next to each name, write one small action you can take to make them feel more connected or valued this week.

1.

_____

2.

_____

3.

_____

"A Change is Gonna Come" – Sam Cooke

| 6 |

Grace in the Journey

Grace in the Journey

D EIB work isn't a sprint or a straight line—it's a winding path full of detours, lessons, and moments of growth. Along this journey, grace is essential. It's about being kind to yourself and others, understanding that mistakes will happen, and continuing to move forward with courage and compassion.

Playlist Song: "Don't Stop Believin'" – Journey

What is Grace in DEIB Work?

Grace is the willingness to forgive yourself and others for not having all the answers while staying committed to learning and improving. Growth requires patience, reflection, and the courage to keep going, even when the path is hard to see.

In DEIB work, progress is often more important than perfection. Small, consistent steps build momentum. Grace allows us to stumble, reflect, and try again.

A Global Perspective on Grace and Growth

Across the globe, cultures teach us how to embrace the journey of growth with patience and grace:

1. **Ubuntu (South Africa):**
   Ubuntu, a Nguni Bantu term, means "I am because we are." It emphasizes interconnection and the importance of community in personal growth. This philosophy teaches that we grow through supporting one another and finding shared humanity.

   ◦ **Source:** Tutu, D. (1999). *No Future Without Forgiveness.* Image.

2. **Kaizen (Japan):**

Kaizen is a Japanese concept meaning "continuous improvement." It focuses on achieving growth through small, consistent steps rather than grand leaps, reminding us that progress is a journey, not a destination.

   ○ **Source:** Imai, M. (1986). *Kaizen: The Key to Japan's Competitive Success.* McGraw-Hill Education.

3. **Hózhó (Navajo Nation):**

Hózhó refers to the Navajo philosophy of harmony, balance, and beauty. It teaches that challenges are part of life's balance, and embracing them allows us to grow while maintaining spiritual and emotional harmony.

   ○ **Source:** Farella, J. R. (1990). *The Main Stalk: A Synthesis of Navajo Philosophy.* University of Arizona Press.

Dr. Shawn Wilson (2008) emphasizes that learning and growth are relational processes. True progress happens through connection, reflection, and shared accountability.

"The journey of growth is about relationship: with ourselves, with others, and with the work we do."

Think about this connection. Grace requires us to approach challenges relationally, understanding that progress comes from collaboration and mutual support.

A Path in Australia

At a school in Sydney, a teacher introduced restorative circles to address conflicts in the classroom. In the first few sessions, students struggled to open up, and the process felt awkward.

Instead of giving up, the teacher reflected on her approach and sought feedback from the students. By adjusting the process and modeling vulnerability, the circles became spaces of trust and growth.

The teacher shared, "I realized that the journey itself was the lesson. Each step we took together made us stronger as a group."

Reflection:

What challenges have you faced in your DEIB journey? How have those challenges helped you grow?

Next Steps

This week, practice showing yourself and others grace. Whether it's forgiving a mistake, taking a break to reflect, or celebrating a small win, remember: progress is the goal, not perfection.

Playlist Song: "Don't Stop Believin'" – Journey

The Path to Progress

Goal: Help you to reflect on your journey, embrace mistakes as part of growth, and think about how you can practice grace for yourself and others.

Instructions:

Imagine Your Path:
Close your eyes and think of your DEIB journey as a winding path. It's not a straight line—it has twists, turns, and detours.
Along the way, you've picked up tools, encountered challenges, and shared moments of connection.

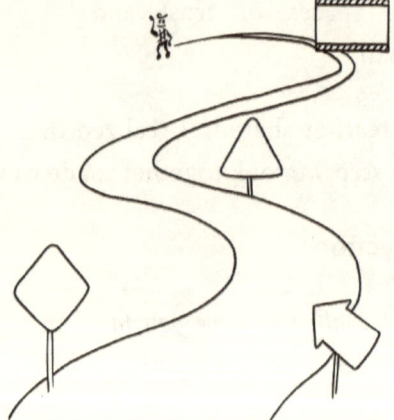

Map Your Path:

- Use the space below to draw, write, or doodle your journey.

- Mark key moments:
  - **A detour:** A mistake or challenge that taught you something.

  - **A milestone:** A moment of progress or growth.

  - **A helping hand:** Someone who supported you along the way.

Reflection Questions:

- What did you learn from your detours?

- How do your milestones remind you of your progress?

- Who has been a part of your journey, and how can you show them gratitude?

My DEIB Path

Pack Your Backpack

What tools do you need for the next stage of your journey?

1. Draw a backpack below.
2. Fill it with "tools" that will help you keep moving forward. These tools could be:

   - **Skills**: Patience, active listening, vulnerability.
   - **People**: Mentors, colleagues, friends.
   - **Resources**: Books, podcasts, workshops.

Reflection Prompt:

What's one "tool" you've gained on your journey so far? How has it helped you grow?

What's one "tool" you wish you had? How can you work toward finding or building it?

_____

_____

_____

_____

_____

Think about someone else's journey. Write down one way you can show them grace this week:

- A supportive conversation.
- A gesture of encouragement.
- A shared moment of vulnerability.

_____

_____

_____

Playlist Song: "Don't Stop Believin'" – Journey

| 7 |

Conclusion: The Final Chorus

The Final Chorus

Your Journey is Just Beginning

As you reach the end of this book, take a moment to pause and reflect. You've stepped into this journey of diversity, equity, inclusion, and belonging not because it's easy, but because it's meaningful.

This book may be coming to a close, but your journey is just beginning. Each page you've read, each reflection you've written, and each activity you've completed has been a step toward creating a more inclusive, connected, and harmonious world.

Stepping Onto the Stage

Imagine a stage with a microphone under a bright spotlight. That microphone is yours. Your voice, your actions, and your choices have the power to inspire change. Whether you're leading a classroom, guiding a team, or taking steps in your personal life, your impact matters.

You don't have to know every answer or have every step mapped out. What matters is that you show up, ready to listen, learn, and grow.

A Gift for Your Next Step

To support you on your continued journey, I'm offering a free 20-minute coaching session. This is your time to:

- Reflect on your personal growth.
- Gain clarity on your next steps.
- Ask questions or brainstorm ideas for your organization or community.

Use this session for yourself or share it with your organization—it's my way of walking this path with you.

Scan Here to Schedule Your Free Coaching Session

Final Reflection Questions

1. *What's one key takeaway from this book that you'll carry forward?*
2. *What's one action you'll take this week to build bridges in your environment?*
3. *Who can you invite to join you on this journey?*

_____

_____

_____

_____

_____

_____

_____

One Love, One Step at a Time

As Bob Marley reminds us, "One love, one heart, let's get together and feel all right." Change happens when we come together with intention, care, and action. Your voice, your heart, and your steps are what will make this journey meaningful—not just for yourself, but for everyone around you.

Thank you for showing up. Thank you for choosing to build bridges. Let's keep walking this path together.

Playlist Song: "One Love" – Bob Marley

Take the Stage

Goal: Empower you to reflect on your journey through the book and commit to actionable steps moving forward.

Instructions:

Imagine you're stepping onto a stage, with the spotlight shining on you. This is your moment to share your DEIB vision with the world. What would you say? Who's in your audience? What impact do you want to leave?

1. **Reflection Prompts:**

    ○ *What is one thing you've learned from this book that surprised or challenged you?*
    ○ *What message do you want to share with others about DEIB?*
    ○ *Who do you want to invite to join you on this journey?*

_____

_____

_____

_____

_____

_____

2. **Task: Write Your Final Chorus**

   ○ Write a short speech, statement, or even lyrics for your "final chorus" to share with your audience. Use this as a way to summarize your vision for building bridges and creating a more inclusive world.

   _____

   _____

   _____

   _____

   _____

   _____

   _____

Your Stage

Your Call to Action

Schedule Your Coaching Session:
Use the QR code below to schedule your free 20-minute coaching session. Whether it's for personal growth or to brainstorm ideas for your organization, this session is your next step on the journey.

Reflection Questions:

- What's one action you will take this week to build bridges in your community?
- How will you hold yourself accountable for continuing this work?

_____

_____

_____

_____

_____

Playlist Song: "One Love" – Bob Marley

Closing Thought:
The spotlight is yours. Take the stage with confidence, grace, and the knowledge that every step you take makes a difference.

References

Scholarly Works

1. Farella, J. R. (1990). *The Main Stalk: A Synthesis of Navajo Philosophy.* University of Arizona Press.
2. Hau'ofa, E. (1994). *Our Sea of Islands.* The Contemporary Pacific, 6(1), 148-161.
3. Imai, M. (1986). *Kaizen: The Key to Japan's Competitive Success.* McGraw-Hill Education.
4. Ladson-Billings, G. (1995). *Toward a Theory of Culturally Relevant Pedagogy.* American Educational Research Journal, 32(3), 465-491.
5. Moreton-Robinson, A. (2015). *The White Possessive: Property, Power, and Indigenous Sovereignty.* University of Minnesota Press.
6. Muhammad, G. (2020). *Cultivating Genius: An Equity Framework for Culturally and Historically Responsive Literacy.* Scholastic.
7. powell, j. a. (2012). *Racing to Justice: Transforming Our Conceptions of Self and Other to Build an Inclusive Society.* Indiana University Press.
8. Tutu, D. (1999). *No Future Without Forgiveness.* Image.
9. Wilson, S. (2008). *Research is Ceremony: Indigenous Research Methods.* Fernwood Publishing.

Music Playlist

1. Withers, B. (1972). *Lean on Me.* On *Still Bill* [Album]. Sussex Records.

2. Sister Sledge. (1979). *We Are Family.* On *We Are Family* [Album]. Cotillion Records.

3. Jackson, M. (1988). *Man in the Mirror.* On *Bad* [Album]. Epic Records.

4. Williams, P. (2013). *Happy.* On *G I R L* [Album]. Columbia Records.

5. Cooke, S. (1964). *A Change is Gonna Come.* On *Ain't That Good News* [Album]. RCA Victor.

6. Journey. (1981). *Don't Stop Believin'.* On *Escape* [Album]. Columbia Records.

7. Marley, B. (1984). *One Love/People Get Ready.* On *Legend* [Album]. Island Records.

 **Marla Hunter [Hooper]** is an educator, author, and global consultant who is passionate about fostering human connection through storytelling, leadership, and cultural awareness. With a strong background in education and professional development, she has worked with individuals and organizations worldwide to create learning environments that inspire growth, inclusivity, and meaningful engagement.

As the founder of Live. Love. Teach!, LLC, Marla specializes in curriculum development, leadership training, and instructional design, helping educators and professionals build bridges across cultures and experiences. Her writing blends personal narratives, research, and actionable strategies to empower readers to cultivate spaces of belonging, purpose, and transformation.

A lifelong lover of music, culture, and education, Marla infuses these passions into her work, demonstrating how love and leadership intersect to create lasting impact. When she's not writing or consulting, she enjoys exploring global cultures, sharing knowledge, and inspiring others to embrace lifelong learning.

For more information, visit **www.msmarlahunter.com** and **www.learnwithmarla.com**

Stephanie Gowdy also known as Alyrical is a legally blind visual artist born and raised in South Florida. As an artist, Alyrical works with acrylic on canvas along with mixed media graphite, watercolor pencils and charcoal on paper for portraits.

Despite her many struggles in life such as being diagnosed with epilepsy, and keratoconus causing her to lose her sight. Alyrical knows God didn't take her sight to disable her, rather He took her site so she could clearly see the purpose for which He created her. Alyrical continues to use her inner vision and lives out her purpose by being a visual artist.

Alyrical's position is that art can be for everyone, using it to not only create awareness for multiple topics but bring society together.

One of her favorite bible verses is Proverbs 29:18 "where there is no vision people perish." Alyrical refuses to allow her life setbacks, health issues, or the loss of her sight to stop her sharing her vision and inspiring others to follow their dreams.

You can follow Alyrical on Instagram visit **https://www.instagram.com/itsalyrical/**

Fun Fact: Stephanie is Marla's couster (cousin-sister)!

www.ingramcontent.com/pod-product-compliance
Lightning Source LLC
Chambersburg PA
CBHW020810130626
46554CB00006B/2360